# Become You

## *Using Spiritual Energy To Transform Your Life!*

By

Kelly Wallace

Professional Psychic Counselor

[DrKellyPsychic.com](http://DrKellyPsychic.com/)

©2014, 2017, 2021 All Rights Reserved

*Intuitive Living Publishing*

# Table of Contents

Copyright Page .................................................................... 1

Books by Kelly Wallace ....................................................... 4

About Kelly Wallace ............................................................ 7

Introduction ......................................................................... 8

~ Part One ~ ....................................................................... 10

Why You're Stuck ............................................................. 11

Spiritual Energy ................................................................. 14

Finding Your Spiritual Energy ........................................ 16

Learning To Focus ............................................................ 21

Increasing Spiritual Energy .............................................. 24

Mind Mastery .................................................................... 31

Spiritual Protection .......................................................... 36

Spiritual Awakening ......................................................... 40

~ Part Two ~ ...................................................................... 47

Love Yourself .................................................................... 48

How We Ruin Relationships ........................................... 54

- Soulmate Relationships .................................................. 59
- Spiritual Sexuality ........................................................... 65
- Strengthen Your Relationship ....................................... 68
- Money Energy ................................................................ 72
- Physical Energy .............................................................. 78
- ~ Part Three ~ ................................................................. 83
- Letting Go Of Fear ........................................................ 84
- Enjoying Your Life ......................................................... 86
- Getting What You Want ................................................ 92
- Living Your Dreams ....................................................... 95
- Finding Your Life Purpose ............................................ 99
- Contact Me/Book A Reading ...................................... 101

# Books by Kelly Wallace

---

10 Minutes A Day to A Powerful New Life

Become Your Higher Self – Using Spiritual Energy to Transform Your Life

Breaking The Worry Habit – Stop Your Anxious Thoughts And Start Living!

Chakras – Heal, Clear, And Strengthen Your Energy Centers

Clear Your Karma – The Healing Power of Your Past Lives

Contacting Your Spirit Guides – Meeting and Working with Your Invisible Helpers

Creating A Charmed Life – Enchantments to Attract, Repel, Cleanse & Heal

Dream Work – Using The Wisdom Of Your Sleeping Mind To Change Your Waking Life

Energy Work – Heal, Cleanse, and Strengthen Your Aura

Everyday Miracles – Powerful Steps to Wonderful Experiences

Finding Your Life Purpose – Uncover Your Soul's True Goals

Healing the Child Within – Rewrite Your Early Childhood Life Script

How to Cure Candida – Yeast Infection Symptoms, Causes, Diet & Natural Remedies

Intuitive Living – Developing Your Psychic Gifts

Intuitive Tarot – Learn the Tarot Instantly

Is He The One? Finding And Keeping Your Soulmate

Master the Art of Picking Up Women

Master the Art of Dating Women

Master the Art of Sex and Seduction

Never Good Enough – Escaping The Prison Of Perfectionism

No-Sweat Homeschooling – The Cheap, Free, and Low-Stress Way to Teach Your Kids

Psychic Vampires – Protect and Heal Yourself from Energy Predators

Reclaiming Your Soul – Healing Your Spirit, Building Confidence, & Finding Your Voice

Reprogram Your Subconscious – Use The Power Of Your Mind

Signs From The Universe – How To Recognize And Interpret These Life-Changing Messages

Spirit Guides And Healing Energy – Worth Your Guides, Aura, and Chakras

Spirits I Have Known – Haunted Places, Haunted People

Spiritual Alchemy – Transform Your Life and Everyone In It

The Art Of Happiness – Living A Life Of Peace And Simplicity

The Love You Deserve – Release Toxic Relationships and Attract Your Soulmate

The Mended Soul – Healing Your Mind, Body, & Spirit From Anxiety & Depression

The Overwhelmed Empath – A Guide For Sensitive Souls

The Power of Pets – How to Psychically Communicate with Your Pet

Transforming Your Money Mindset – From Broke To Abundance

True Wealth – Reprogram Your Subconscious for Financial Success

Upgrade Your Life – Small Changes, Easy Actions, Big Success

Way Of The Lightworker – Discovering Your Role & Following Your Path

Working With Your Angels – Contact Your Loving Guardians

# About Kelly Wallace

Kelly is a bestselling spiritual and self-help author, former radio show host, and has been a professional psychic counselor for over twenty years. She can see, hear, sense, and feel information sent from Spirit, the Universe, and a client's Higher Self.

She offers professional psychic counseling, caring guidance, and solutions that work! More than just a typical psychic reading or counseling session, you will feel you've found a real friend during your time of need—whether you simply want answers and guidance to your current worries or concerns, or you're interested in learning more about your soulmate, spirit guides, angels, past lives, or anything else.

Contact her today for an in-depth and life-altering reading!

Website: DrKellyPsychic.com

Email: Dr.Kelly.Psychic.Counselor@gmail.com

# Introduction

What is spiritual energy? How important is it? How can you harness this invisible power and live a happier, more successful life?

For twenty-plus years I've been a psychic counselor offering guidance on everything from auras and past lives to soul mates and spirit guides. I've covered careers and lost love, life purpose and health issues, fertility and death, religious uncertainties, and have even helped with a few scientific breakthroughs. One of the main things I stress to my clients is to work on strengthening their own spiritual energy. This is the only way to become your higher self and achieve your desires.

So many people have problems with money, health, love, and happiness. We feel tired, depressed, uninspired, and life is one long treadmill. All of this could be easily solved if we spent more time working with our spiritual energy rather than wasting time on thoughts and activities that get us nowhere.

The problem is, since spiritual energy can't be seen or felt like mental, physical, and emotional energy, people are under the false impression that spiritual energy is bogus or too difficult to master. Within these pages, I'll cover some of the most important topics clients come to me about. These are the same subjects nearly everyone on the planet struggles with: Personal power, love, and money.

Can you imagine how confident and free you would feel if you could erase such problems as depression, anxiety, fatigue, negative relationships, and financial problems? Not only is this possible, but nearly guaranteed once you understand what spiritual energy is and how to work with it.

This type of energy is incredibly powerful and can have you feeling and living in the depths of despair or at a high level of joy and wealth. How do I know this? For decades, I barely scraped by with my finances and went from one negative relationship to another. I felt that this was just how life was...until I had a spiritual awakening. Once that happened I knew, *really knew*, that I had complete control over my present and future. Life could be everything I ever dreamed of!

My goal in writing this book is to guide you along your own spiritual energy path and help you to experience an awakening that will change absolutely everything you currently think, feel, and live. Life doesn't have to remain stagnant and you don't have to accept less than what you deserve, dream, and desire. You *can* become your higher self!

I'm all about keeping things simple, so I won't go into any deep esoteric ramblings. In my opinion, too many spiritual authors make things seem far more complicated than they need to be, or push you in the direction of a certain religion or lifestyle. That's completely unnecessary. Spiritual energy is as logical as mental, physical, and emotional energy.

Let's get started on your spiritual path to personal transformation!

# ~ Part One ~

———

*Personal Energy*

# Why You're Stuck

Unless you're operating at a strong level of spiritual energy, life will be stuck in one or more areas. Everyone and everything is made up of energy. Where you're at right now in life is the direct result of how your spiritual energy is or isn't flowing. If your life is negative or lacking in some way then it's a sure sign that you've got energy blockages.

These blockages hold you back from experiencing the true happiness you yearn for. It keeps you in negative relationships, struggling financially, and riddled with health problems. It keeps you confused, numb, and frustrated, living at the level of your lower self rather than your natural higher self.

Your true state of being should be a life where you experience feelings of joy, your thoughts are clear, and your emotions are balanced. Love and positive opportunities should flow freely toward you. In turn, your energy should flow outward, taking advantage of those opportunities and offering love in return.

This doesn't mean that at this point in your life you constantly live on the brink of ruin and despair, but life simply won't work as it should if you're clogged up with negative energy. Over time, if one area of your life is blocked then ultimately it will affect all other areas.

For example, have you ever come into a lump sum of money, or perhaps fallen madly in love, only to have it quickly disappear?

It's not the fact that you have bad luck or aren't deserving, it's because you aren't working with your spiritual self correctly.

*Baby Steps*

Your first step to becoming your higher self is to be completely honest with yourself about where you're at in life right now. Acceptance is the foundation of release. When you fight against what is, it creates a huge block that holds back all those wonderful things you see other people experiencing.

Look at your surroundings right now and look inside yourself. What do you see? Is your home cluttered? Are your thoughts just as cluttered? Are there items you no longer use or never needed to begin with? Do you hold on to old beliefs that no longer move you forward or were subconsciously programmed by your parents or other adults? Does your mind repeat negative conversations and experiences over and over?

As simple as it sounds, just by clearing out the clutter in your home, closets, garage, and workspace, you're actually taking a huge step toward allowing spiritual energy to flow freely in your life.

You can't live a life of abundance, find your soul mate, or attract money if there's no room for movement. Nothing new can come in if old things are clogging up your home and your mind. It's time to let go of everything you no longer need, of everything holding you back; this includes physical items, people, and past experiences.

As a soul living a human existence, your life purpose is in alignment with where you focus your energy. If all you focus on is the past and keep acquiring junk—junk items, junk food, junk people—how will you ever embrace the life you've fantasized about for so long? How will you get to where you want to be?

You are a being of immense energy, and how you direct that energy touches every area of your life. By the end of this book, you'll know exactly where you want to go and how to get there. In fact, you can become an entirely new person.

# Spiritual Energy

When I talk about spiritual energy, this isn't in a religious sense, it's being in tune with your inner self. It means living a life of passion, conviction, and honesty with yourself and everyone you come in contact with. It's about living a life of purpose.

It doesn't mean you need to sacrifice yourself for others, nor does it mean you should be self-centered. It's finding that balance between committing yourself to those you care about while pursuing your own desires. It's believing in yourself and your abilities to make your life and the lives of others a better place. It's being your higher self.

Once you've been spiritually awakened and are on your true path in life, hard times may still come your way but, you'll weather those storms much easier and will get right back on your desired road regardless of the challenges you face.

Many people, especially women, find it easy to give every ounce of their energy to others: their children, spouse, friends, and so forth. Yet when it comes to concentrating on ourselves we feel guilty or at a loss.

Yes, reaching out to those people and causes you care about creates stability in your life. It helps you to avoid being self-centered and, by giving to others, it makes you feel good on many levels and creates a more positive mindset, helping you face your own personal challenges.

It's easy to go to extremes though and shove your own wants and needs aside as you tend to everyone except yourself. This is why you need to seek balance and spend time working on your spirituality.

# Finding Your Spiritual Energy

---

We've talked about what spiritual energy is and why it's important, but it isn't the same for everyone. There isn't a spiritual blueprint everyone should follow, leading them to a life of bliss. Instead, you need to discover what matters most to *you*. Only then will you become the powerful being you were meant to be.

You can read through the following questions and answer them in your mind or, better yet, write in a journal or open a blank document on your computer and type your thoughts out.

1. *What fills you with spiritual energy?*

Remember, we aren't talking about religion. Your spirituality relates to your connections with people, the planet, and all living things. It's something you enjoy and feel really good about. In turn, this energy goes deep inside you, lighting those internal spiritual fires.

For me, I love being in nature. I live in Baltimore and feel steeped in my own spirituality simply by spending time among the streams and lakes, trees and flowers. Often, I'm filled with such an incredible force I feel like I literally glow from the center of my being. In turn, this force colors my actions and reactions, reaching out and positively affecting everyone around me.

Many activities can fill us with spiritual energy such as volunteering, playing music, dancing, spending time with loved ones, meditating, and so on. Dozens of things fill me with spiritual energy, nature is just one of them. What are some things you love doing?

2. *Who makes you feel most energized?*

Who do you like being around? What is it about her/him that makes you feel this way? Does this person make you feel happy, connected, enlightened, more aware, or optimistic? What traits of this person would you like to incorporate into your own life?

When I was younger I surrounded myself with many people. Some lifted me up while others put me down. Some made me feel light and energized, while others had me feeling drained and depressed. After my spiritual awakening, I realized what a waste it was having people in my life who dragged me down—this included two husbands and a relative! Now I choose to only interact with others who are spiritually energetic.

One person I love having in my life is Cassie. She doesn't even know she's a spiritual person and it doesn't really matter. Our energies complement each other well and we spend time together at least once a week. She faces each problem she encounters with confidence and conviction, and she's one of the most laid-back people I know. Not much ruffles this lady's feathers, and she's always trying to better herself. Once she reaches one rung on life's ladder, she moves on to the next.

A spiritually energizing person leaves you feeling positive after having been in their company.

3. *Who or what makes you feel spiritually drained?*

This is different than feeling physically drained. After a long day of work, of tending to kids, laundry, shopping, or household chores you probably feel physically, mentally, and/or emotionally drained and this can indeed affect you spiritually. What we're talking about here though is what hits you in the spiritual zone. Who or what leaves you feeling like you've got a gaping hole in your soul? Could it be a lack of purpose in life, a negative relationship, or a dead-end job? Maybe someone in your life drains you?

A few things that have spiritually drained me are:

- Living in the desert. I truly needed to be in lush surroundings to feel spiritually energized so I moved back to Baltimore.

- Not following my life purpose. I tried my hand at public speaking and being a ghostwriter. These two things drained me on many levels. Once I started writing my own books and helping others this way my spiritual self grew by leaps and bounds.

- Choosing the wrong men. Since I was used to seeing the men in my life abuse women, I naturally gravitated toward these dysfunctional relationships. Not until I was spiritually awakened did I start to attract positive men.

The interesting thing about your spiritual self is it will know when something is right or wrong before you know it on an emotional, mental or physical level. You get a niggling sensation inside that says this person or situation is bad for you, yet we ignore it until we're affected on other levels.

4. *What are your top five energy boosters?*

What healthy things do you do, or can you do, to make yourself feel more energized? Do you go for a walk, exercise, meditate, read a book, write in a journal, or play a game or sport? This is something personal to you and doesn't necessarily mean you're helping another person. Sure, we associate deep spirituality with reaching out to the world around us, but you need to nurture yourself as well.

When I need an energy boost I either crochet, watch a movie with a loved one, take a walk, play my flute, or listen to music. These small things that bring me pleasure really help to lift me up spiritually. As I mentioned before, everything is connected within you. Something that affects you on one level—be it mentally, physically, emotionally, or spiritually—is going to seep in and affect all other areas.

5. *What or who requires too much spiritual energy at this time?*

Even if something seems like a good cause or worthwhile activity, at this point in your life it might require far too much spiritual energy. Pursuing this activity or relationship may cause you to feel drained, disconnected, or frustrated.

Your spiritual path should fill you with joy and peace. If there's something in your life that isn't contributing to your highest good, ask yourself if you really want to hold on to it.

Sometimes, releasing someone or something is the quickest way to recapture spiritual energy and focus.

A few years ago, I wanted to start volunteering since I knew it would add to my overall happiness and spiritual pursuits. Animals and domestic abuse are two of my top concerns. I went to several animal shelters to see how I could offer my volunteer services, though I quickly discovered it would require far more time and effort than I could comfortably provide.

I didn't want to feel drained or stressed out when I was trying to do the world a bit of good! Finally, I found a few volunteer places that met my personal schedule. I crochet "comfort scarves" for abused women and help with online science projects.

Pursuing a spiritual path should never leave you feeling tired or frustrated. Seek out those people and activities that make you feel fulfilled.

# Learning To Focus

---

Your higher self is always aware and ever-observant, constantly ready to help. As I've talked about, we're truly beings of light inside a physical body. Yes, you need that physical body while living here on the Earth plane, but by learning to master your spiritual energy, life on Earth can be so much more rewarding. This is a technique you can use to become more focused in life and spiritually centered. By allowing your aura to vibrate at a higher frequency, life becomes much different than what you've experienced so far.

1. Go someplace quiet, such as your bedroom, and sit on a chair, the floor, or your bed. For just a minute or so focus on your breathing and allow your body to relax. If you find it hard to relax, focus your attention on your feet, tense them up then consciously relax them. Move your attention to your calves and do the same thing. Repeat for each area of your body, all the way to your face. Tense then relax as you breathe normally.

Once you've finished, you should feel more relaxed than when you first started this exercise, if not, don't worry about it and just move on to the next step. In time, you'll get better and better at relaxing quickly.

If you find your brain is filled with swirling thoughts and mindless chatter, try not to focus on it. Just push the thoughts aside and carry on with this exercise.

2. Now visualize a beam of beautiful white light sent down to you from the Universe, your guides, your angels, or whatever resonates with you. Imagine this light pouring into the top of your head and going to your toes until you're completely filled up with this pure white energy.

3. As this light fills you, imagine any negativity in your body being pushed out through the soles of your feet and going down into the center of the Earth where it's burned up. Or, if you prefer, imagine the negativity leaving your body and your angels or guides taking these problems away from you and healing them.

4. Notice the empty spaces where the negativity used to be and visualize the white light filling those places with love, warmth, and healing. You're released from all negativity as it's replaced with an energy of peace and happiness.

5. When you feel a shift inside you, no matter how small, you are fully cleansed. In the beginning, you might not feel anything but just go through the exercise each day until you're more in tune with your spiritual energy.

Allow yourself to enjoy this feeling of lightness for a few minutes before coming out of the exercise. When you're ready, open your eyes, take a deep breath in through your nose and let it out, then stretch a bit before getting up and moving around.

6. Go through your day and see if things seem different, and if you feel different. Perhaps you find solutions to problems, or life is easier to tackle. Situations that normally bother you

may now barely register as you operate at this level of higher vibration.

The more you use this technique the more benefits you'll see in how you feel and what you experience.

# Increasing Spiritual Energy

---

Your body, like your thoughts, is pure energy, though your thoughts are much more powerful at creating your life than your body is. Why? Because your thoughts have no limitations such as gravity and the material plane. However, since we are beings of pure energy, we affect everything around us and vice versa. *You are literally an energy magnet.*

To show how strong energy is, you've probably walked into a room and, even if the room was completely empty, you sensed energy. Perhaps the vibes you felt were heavy, buzzing, or an eerie void. Since we all emit energy, whatever took place in a room—or anywhere on Earth—saturates the area with energy particles.

The more intense the event, the stronger the energy and the longer the vibrations will hang around, whether a wedding or a war. Unfortunately, it's usually the negative energies that stick around longest since so much emotion is involved.

Not only are locations saturated with energy, but it's within you as well. Everything you think, feel, and eat affects your energy field. It seems logical then that we should surround ourselves with good people and events, and fill ourselves with good (healthy) food and thoughts. In turn, this will allow your spiritual energy to vibrate at a higher rate, helping you to be healthier all around.

*Thoughts Are Powerful*

For just a moment, think about the biggest problem you're facing in life right now. Stay with this negative thought for a minute or so. Now think about something or someone you're grateful for in as much detail as possible. Did you notice how differently you felt when thinking of one compared to the other? Thoughts have vibrations and those vibrations affect your emotions and even your physical body.

I'm sure you've been in this "zone" before: Things are going well in your life, your mood is bright, and you attract positive people and opportunities with ease. Even if this zone lasted only a short while, you felt unstoppable. Imagine if you always lived your life from this place of incredible spiritual energy!

This isn't impossible. In fact, as a spiritual being, this is your natural state. The problem is, we allow our mind and emotions to run our lives rather than operating from a place of spirituality. We overthink and overreact. Soon, life is a mess or completely stagnant.

By learning a few simple meditation and visualization exercises you can reconnect with your spiritual self, shift your energy, and live life from the wondrous place of your higher self. You can do all the exercises together or pick and choose the ones that resonate most with you now. When needed, feel free to do any of the other exercises.

In my own life, I tend to do all five exercises at once before I get out of bed in the morning. It only takes a few minutes, but when I do these I notice I feel more relaxed, confident, and positive. Throughout the day I may need to do one or more of the other exercises. Maybe I've been a bit stressed, so I do the grounding exercise. Perhaps someone negative is talking to me, then I do the *Own Your Energy* exercise. Do what feels right and most comfortable for you.

1. *Center yourself*: As you did in the previous exercise, find a quiet and comfortable place to sit or lie down. Close your eyes and allow yourself to relax for a few minutes, focusing on your breathing and consciously relaxing your body. Once you feel relaxed, center yourself by bringing all your awareness to your third eye which is in the middle of your forehead and back a few inches inside your head. In this space, it should feel peaceful and quiet.

Now move your awareness directly on your forehead. This is the area of your mind where all your thinking and planning takes place. While concentrating on this area you might find it very busy or overwhelming. It's amazing at the constant thoughts whirling around there!

Move back to the center of your head and find that place of peace again. This is where you can work with your higher self and access any information and truths you're seeking. Don't worry if you can't find this quiet center at first. You've gotten used to thinking, worrying, and so much inner chatter that your higher, wiser self is sometimes hard to tap into in the beginning. Don't give up though, your true essence is there.

When you get used to bringing your attention to the center of your mind, you can analyze your life better and make healthier decisions. *You* will be running your life rather than your mind and emotions running *you*. In this space life becomes easier, we become wiser, calmer, more loving, and intuitive.

2. *Ground yourself*: Imagine a white light flowing in through the top of your head, down your spine, out through your feet, and into the center of the Earth. Allow this calming and cleansing white light to fill you, surround you, grounding you to the planet, to the present, and releasing all worries and fears.

Stay with this image for a moment until you feel a sense of peace, a calmness, a subtle shift in energy, a humming sensation, anything different that shows you're grounded and the meditation is working. At first, it might be hard to tell if you're feeling differently, but over time it will become stronger. Even if you feel absolutely nothing, *believe* you're grounded and move to the next step.

3. *Focus on your aura*: This is your natural energy field that exists inside of you and spreads outward. If your aura is very strong it can extend outward several feet, though at first, it will probably only extend an inch or so. Your aura is an electromagnetic field that you see everything through and everyone sees you through. You can think of it as a glass egg or window.

If the window is clear you see life more clearly and pursue goals more easily. If the window is dirty it's difficult to see things easily, decisions and life iitself become muddied, and people can't see the real you. Also, when your aura energy is strong you create healthy boundaries instead of allowing others to deplete your energy or inflict their emotions onto you.

I go into detail on how to work with your aura in my book *Energy Work: Heal, Cleanse, and Strengthen Your Aura*. Right now, I'll share an easy exercise with you. As we've been doing, visualize that white light still pouring down from the Universe and into the top of your head, filling you, expanding outward until it surrounds you. White represents spirituality, cleansing, and renewal. Over time you can choose other colors, but for now, we'll focus on white since it's a great basic color.

Feel the warmth of this comforting light and naturally allow it to grow in intensity. Imagine that you light up, just like a light bulb, and this energy is all around you. In the beginning, you might only feel a slight warmth or movement in your solar plexus and can only visualize a small light. As you get better at working with your spiritual energy you'll find that your aura light becomes stronger and wider, extending far beyond your head and body.

4. *Own your energy*: This is another important step. So often we allow others to take our energy from us. Have you noticed that when you're around certain people they seem to drain you, leaving you tired, depressed, anxious, or irritable? That's because, without realizing it, you're handing over all your spiritual energy to this person. Even focusing intently on a work project can deplete your personal energy.

When you're with a person like this or in a situation that typically drains you, imagine a golden ball of light floating a foot or so above your head. Visualize this golden ball as being a high-powered magnet that only attracts positive energies from the Universe and your guides or angels. Once the golden light seems filled with positive energies bring it down through the top of your head and allow this golden light to spread throughout your entire body and organs. Then imagine the light flowing around you like a protective egg extending a foot or more around your body. Soon, you should feel more confident and relaxed.

5. *Your higher self:* Now that you've worked on creating a stronger aura and owning your spiritual energy, I want you to allow your higher self to focus on your mind, body, and emotions. Don't think about anything too much and don't allow your lower Earth self to get involved. Simply act as if you were an angel or spirit guide looking you over and finding areas that are heavy or dark.

Mentally scan every part of your body, inside and out. When you find an area that's out of sync with your higher self, send light to it—either white or gold—until you feel the area shift. Imagine that cold, wounded, worried, or empty part of yourself being light as a feather and filled with your aura energy.

A while back I had a bad fall and broke my ankle and wrist. As an author, typing is a huge part of my day, but my previously wounded wrist constantly protests. I've been to physical therapy and everything is fine, it's just that my mind remembers the wrist was hurt and it doesn't want me to use it. My mind is trying to protect me, but really there's no need for it. I'm healed and fine.

However, at this moment after typing so much it feels painful. So, what I'll do right now is focus on the sore area and shift my spiritual energy, bringing warm, golden light to my wrist. I'll visualize the light soothing the area, strengthening it, relaxing it, and removing the pain. All it takes is a few seconds and no more than a minute. Just now I took a moment to do the exercise and, believe it or not, the pain is gone. It's amazing to know how strong our energy really is and the things it's capable of.

Once you've done one or more of the previous exercises, simply open your eyes, take a deep breath in then out, and stretch a bit before getting up.

Every moment of every day you're creating your own reality. I can't stress that enough: *You are creating your own reality*! Just by following those five tips, you can learn to become more aware of your spiritual energy, strengthen it, shift it, and operate at a high level of awareness for a healthier, happy life.

# Mind Mastery

---

As a spiritual being, it stands to reason that you should learn how to recognize situations that deplete you. Many people worry about protecting resources such as water, food, money, electricity, and so forth, but we seldom think about protecting our spiritual energy.

Negative thoughts are one of the biggest energy drains because at those times you're giving your energy away. You're handing your energy over to your problems, your fears, and your worries. How will that help anything or anyone? It simply leaves you feeling tired or frustrated, with no way out.

When you're faced with stress it's incredibly important to conserve your spiritual energy so you can quickly and efficiently take care of the situation. The more positive energy you're filled with, the better you can handle life and the more life brings to you. The bottom line is, *thoughts have power*. By choosing your thoughts you choose the direction of your life and the intensity of your spiritual power.

It may seem like thoughts float around in your mind without any conscious effort on your part. Many times, no matter how hard you try, it feels like the thoughts won't stop. You're a victim of your own mind! The truth is, mastering your mind can be as easy as turning the channel on your television. If you don't like a show will you sit there and force yourself to stare at it until it's over? Of course not. You grab the remote and switch channels, finding something you like. Your mind is this way.

Let's look at two situations and how they can be handled:

You finally save some money and your car breaks down, requiring expensive repairs and depleting your savings account. Instantly your mind will kick in and start talking to you. Depending on where you're at spiritually will dictate how this conversation goes.

*Lower self scenario—*

"Every time I try to save money something terrible happens! I'll never get ahead financially so why keep trying? Other people have it so easy. Why is my life so incredibly hard?" This instantly depletes your energy levels and leaves you feeling helpless and hopeless. You're in victim mode.

*Higher self scenario—*

"It's a good thing I had money saved up so I can get these car repairs done. I'm confident things will go well and I'll continue to put money in my savings account. I'm financially responsible and deserve a life of true wealth!" This mindset shows you're in charge, your energy field is strong, and positive things will indeed keep coming your way. Since you've become your higher self you'll recognize good opportunities and pursue goals that get you where you want to be.

Things happen in life and we all hit speed bumps, roadblocks, and even mountains that stand in the way. It's how we handle them that counts. Thoughts have power—yes, I'll say it again and again—so much so that they directly influence your energy field, thereby affecting how you handle life and all that comes your way.

*Mind mastery is a seven-step process:*

1. Get into the habit of paying attention to your thoughts. What self-talk is going on right now inside your head? Are you putting yourself down? Worrying? Confused? Angry? Blank?

2. Practice mindfulness, refusing to get wrapped up in those runaway thoughts that try to throw you off course. Acknowledge the thoughts, thank them for the warning, but gently push them aside allowing your higher-self to take over and lead the way.

3. When a seemingly important or persistent thought pops into your mind, ask yourself if it will help move you forward or hold you back. We typically operate out of fear of the unknown or negative lessons we've learned in the past. The mind, trying to protect you, holds you back so you won't face failure, though the past is gone and no longer serves you.

4. If a negative thought comes to you say the word "stop!" either out loud or in your mind. Negative thoughts become habit and wear grooves along your neural pathways. By getting into a new habit of interrupting the negative thoughts you can replace them with positive thoughts that will actually get you somewhere.

Soon, the positive thoughts create new, strong neural pathways and *those* thoughts become habit. How nice would that be to have a mind filled with loving, confident, exciting thoughts?

5. If a helpful thought comes to you, stay with it for a while. What does it have to tell you? What lessons can you learn, wisdom to be gained, or ideas to pursue? It seems we operate from this level where fear guides us rather than allowing our higher selves to come through and offer help. Who would you want leading you along your life path, a frightened child or a wise master?

6. Believe in your new, positive thoughts. This isn't always easy, especially if you've faced a lot of negativity in life. What you might want to do is make a list of ten positive thoughts such as, "I'm healthy, happy, and loved." "I make wise decisions and act upon them." "I'm great at managing my money and living a life of true wealth." Write these down in the present tense as if you're already living these future truths.

Every time a negative thought nags you, take your list out and read what you've written down, repeating each one out loud if you can. By reading your words and hearing your voice, you're helping those positive traits get in deeper where they can become your reality.

7. Let more wonder into your life. Rather than automatically thinking a situation is negative—such as losing your job or breaking an arm—allow your spiritual self to wonder about it. What lesson does this situation have to teach you? What can you get out of the event that may not be visible to you now?

I mentioned a bit ago that I had fallen, breaking my ankle and wrist. Since I now tend to wonder about situations rather than worrying about them, I asked my higher self what there was to learn from this. I felt like I lived a pretty good life filled with solid financial decisions, surrounded by friends and loved ones, and a career I'm passionate about.

The deeper I looked though I realized I had gotten into a comfortable rut and had completely ignored other things I had intended to do. Long ago I had written down things I wanted to pursue, but had forgotten about. Since my ankle and wrist were in casts, I couldn't get out of the house much, so I had lots of time at home. What did I do?

I researched my family tree all the back to the year 1130, tried my skills at extreme couponing—not my cup of tea, I soon discovered—began taking classes, and got my ebooks into paperback. Had I not gotten injured, I never would have pursued these paths.

Getting into the habit of wondering rather than worrying can mean the difference between living more spiritually or allowing your lower Earth self to take over and keep you stuck.

# Spiritual Protection

---

Everyone needs spiritual protection, though many seek out the professional help of a psychic to do so. Sometimes these psychics charge a hefty sum of money to do something you should be doing for yourself!

I'll never forget one client I had years ago. He had already spent thousands of dollars on several different psychics, hoping to find protection from the bad luck he felt he always encountered. I didn't want to take money from him since I wanted to teach him a lesson that would change his life. *I showed him how to protect himself,* and right now I want to show you how to protect yourself.

Negative energy is always around. Even when you're feeling on top of the world, filled with joy and absolute contentment, negative energy is right there beside you. The only reason it doesn't affect you when you're happy and confident is because your spiritual energy is vibrating higher than the negative energy and you're naturally protected. Pretty interesting, don't you think?

You'd be surprised at how much negativity floats around—everything from the negative feelings of other people, to negative events and lost spirits.

So how do you know if you're being affected by the negative energy around you rather than your own thoughts and feelings? Symptoms may include: sudden feelings of anger, fear, sadness, guilt, depression, anxiety, nightmares, and relationship or work problems. You could also experience physical symptoms such as stomach pains, headaches, cravings, or lack of appetite. You might feel you aren't in your body, like you're spaced-out, feel fatigued, or have poor memory or concentration.

Although these symptoms seem like things you could experience anyway, regardless of negative energies floating around you, the symptoms come on suddenly and with no fault in your own life. It comes out of the blue.

One of the times I experienced this was when I was reading recipes in a cookbook. That sounds like a pretty ordinary activity, right? I felt light in spirit, enjoying looking through the pages, when suddenly a feeling of worry and sadness swept over me. My brain kicked into high gear wondering if something was wrong with one of my daughters.

I called each one and they were fine. I was nearing a panic attack and couldn't figure out why! It then came to me that a negative energy wave was passing through and it actually had nothing to do with me personally. I spent a few minutes meditating then went for a walk around the block. At last, the dark cloud passed and I was back to normal, just like that!

*How do we attract negative energy?*

In my example above I was just in the wrong place at the wrong time. My mind was in a receptive state since I was reading and not paying attention to my surroundings and as that negative energy came through it temporarily attached itself to me. If I hadn't figured out what it was and acted I could have worried about it, allowing it to attach itself even stronger and hang around much longer.

Other ways you can pick up negative energy is anything that weakens your aura such as being in an abusive relationship, taking drugs, drinking too much alcohol, not eating properly, anything extremely emotional, illness, injury, and surgery. These situations almost guarantee that a negative cloud will find you and stick around until you rid yourself of it. Like attracts like.

*So how do you protect or clear yourself of this negative energy?*

Obviously, we should practice healthy habits such as eating right, getting some exercise every day, meditating a few minutes each day, and avoiding excessive alcohol and any drug use except whatever is prescribed by your doctor. You also need to avoid negative people since their energy will cling to you like sticky cobwebs. That's not always easy since you may work with or be related to someone negative.

One of the best ways to protect yourself is to mentally surround yourself with the protective white light we talked about earlier. It's not enough to only do the exercise I walked you through and be done with it, but you must think of this white light several times a day, especially when you feel mentally or physically "off" in any way.

Visualize the light surrounding you, protecting you, warding off all negativity. Ask your guides, angels, or the Universe for assistance and guidance, as well as protection. At this point let it all go and know you're protected. Spiritual confidence is a powerful thing.

If you feel negative energy around your home, burning incense or sage can help clear it out. I burn incense daily, asking my guides for protection and to help dissolve any negative energy hanging around.

Negative energy isn't as scary as most people believe, it just means you're spiritually sensitive and attract negative energy more than others might. And, negative energy is not a permanent or scary thing, though it can be annoying while it's around. There's negativity around always, but how you deal with it and protect yourself is what counts.

# Spiritual Awakening

---

Isn't this what most of us strive for? That one grand moment, or a collection of smaller moments, that have you seeing life and everything in it from a totally different perspective? A place where you can finally live life as your higher self?

Sometimes walking a spiritual path can be very lonely. Not many people are brave enough to reach for their spiritual gifts let alone embrace them and live life from this place every day. In my own life, there were many times when I questioned my intuition and never followed it, refusing to trust in my higher-self, my own spiritual energy.

After a while, I realized how ridiculous this was. I wanted to be happy, healthy, and financially well off. It was obvious my spiritual-self knew how to get there, but my fearful Earth-self had a hard time trusting. Once I did learn to trust though life changed dramatically for me.

But another odd thing happened; I lost many friends. They felt I was no longer the same person, and they were right, I wasn't! I was pursuing the life of my dreams and, since like attracts like, I began attracting other people who were successful and spiritual while old friends drifted away. Rather than feeling sad or angry, I accepted this, knowing I was going through a growing phase.

I haven't regretted a single moment of embracing my true essence. Though, like physical and emotional growth, it comes with pain and loss. Unfortunately, I didn't know anyone else at the time who had gone through a spiritual awakening so I felt very confused, emotional, and sometimes afraid. Spirituality is so much bigger than our Earth-selves that it can often be overwhelming if you aren't sure what's going on. You feel like you're going crazy, not realizing you're waking up on a spiritual level.

How do you know if you're having a spiritual awakening? Here are the top ten signs to look out for. They shouldn't be confused with anything that requires medical help, these are purely spiritual-based symptoms that can show up mentally, emotionally, or even physically.

1. A dramatic change or shift in sleep patterns, libido, career, food preferences, and/or relationships.

2. A surge in creativity and energy pushing you to detoxify your body, de-clutter your home, begin a project you had wanted to do but previously put off, and simplifying your life.

3. Loss of interest in things you used to enjoy and a desire to pursue something else.

4. Yearning for more freedom or excitement.

5. Depression, fatigue, headaches, anxiety, panic attacks, hot flashes, "hearing voices", a sensation of someone being in the room with you.

6. Problems with electric items such as static coming from the TV or radio, lights flickering or going out, touching things and producing static electricity far more than usual.

7. Experiencing an increase in intuition, psychic abilities, coincidences, and/or synchronicities.

8. Heightened awareness of your own thoughts, feelings, and actions. Feeling more in tune with or aware of others' responses, their body language, and their emotions.

9. Sudden healing of your mind, body, or emotions. For example, an episode in your past may have bothered you a great deal for many years and suddenly it no longer has power over you.

10. Current friends or loved ones seem to be drifting away or acting strange around you, even angry or frustrated.

These are common symptoms I've experienced myself and many of my clients have mentioned after we've realized we've gone through a tremendous spiritual growth spurt. I'd like to discuss two of the symptoms in more detail and why they happen.

*Anxiety or Panic Attacks*

When changes occur, we tend to fight against them. As creatures of habit, we like things to stay the same, even if we want to be happier and healthier. When spiritual growth takes place, it happens at a deep level, affecting your emotions, your mind, and body.

You might not understand why you start feeling odd, why you begin experiencing panic attacks or anxiety, you may break out in a sweat and start having nightmares or unable to sleep well.

The reason this happens is because your higher self is trying to help you heal and grow. Anxiety and the other symptoms I just talked about pop up because you're resisting the clearing process.

You sense that changes are taking place and some part of your mind and emotions rebel against it. Your soul wants to be whole and aligned, but when the fragmented parts of yourself rise to the surface either to be healed or released, we sense it as danger and react accordingly.

How should you handle it? When you feel this anxiety rising remind yourself that it's fragmented energy flowing through you and it will soon pass. Take a deep breath and visualize the white or gold light filling you as we practiced with earlier.

Send the healing energy to any places within you that feel particularly dark or off in some way. Repeat to yourself, "I allow my energy to change for my highest good. I live my life from a place of love, success, and happiness. Life is peaceful. Life is simple."

You could notice your energy shifting to a higher, more positive vibrational state right away, or it might take days or even weeks. It all depends on the amount of healing taking place inside, how confident you are with your spiritual process, and how deep of an awakening you experience.

Your spiritual awakening could be significant or happen all at once, though this is rare. Usually, it comes in phases throughout time. I've had a few larger ones with many small ones in between.

At times, an anxiety attack may be due to your aura field suddenly vibrating at such a high frequency that you need to find a way to slow it down a bit. A few good ways to release this pent-up energy are to go for a walk, dance, sing, exercise, or meditate.

I can't tell you how many times I've woken up in the middle of the night or stopped what I was doing and sang at the top of my lungs (even if it has to be in my mind if I'm out in public!) to calm my anxiety and allow my higher self to take the driver's seat. Ugh, how often does your anxiety try to lead the way? Mine has, a lot!

*Physical Sensations*

Although it should be natural for us to live as spiritual beings of light in a physical body, this is rarely the case. We often forget, and some people never realize, that the physical self is merely a temporary house and the soul goes on forever. When you experience spiritual growth the old cellular structures shift, change, and even dissolve, making way for newer, lighter cell structures.

Learning to align the physical body and spiritual self can be uncomfortable if you don't know how to handle it. Once you have enough cells vibrating at a higher rate, you'll feel better than you have in years, or ever.

In the meantime, though you can experience detox symptoms, very much like flu symptoms, along with fatigue, headaches, and fuzzy thinking. You may notice that your scalp or skin tingles, you feel a sudden rush of heat or cold throughout your body, along with aches and painful nerve flashes.

If you experience pain or aching sensations, this could be an area of your body where the energy is blocked or stuck. Persistent headaches can point to the third eye opening up, while stomach aches or a heavy feeling in your chest can relate to feelings you haven't faced and healed. Pain in the legs can show you're unsure of what path to take in life or you feel held back in some way. A chronic cough or sore throat often relates to something that needs to be said to someone but you haven't yet.

Other physical sensations that might pop up when you're meditating are certain parts of your body tingle or feel warm. You could also feel as if you're floating outside of your body. As I got better at aligning my physical and spiritual self, I noticed that when I meditated my soul would suddenly become huge, unable to fit inside my body.

Some ways to handle physical changes and sensations are through yoga, acupuncture, massage, aromatherapy, Epsom salt baths, and music. I've found that listening to or playing music that intuitively aligns with my soul helps me to feel calm while reducing pain and anxiety.

When I was going through a spiritual growth episode that was particularly big I had daily headaches. Nothing to rush off to the doctor or emergency room over, but enough to bother me and affect my mood, energy levels, and thoughts.

I studied aromatherapy and used geranium oil, just a drop massaged into my temples, and it worked wonders. Holistic therapies are much gentler than other therapies, thereby helping you to heal and become stronger in more subtle ways so all levels of your being can work together.

When you experience spiritual growth, you need to be very aware of your thoughts and your self-talk. Because you're changing at such a fast rate, you have more power than you realize. It's at these times that negative self-talk and actions make the most impact and can undo everything you've been working toward.

When you catch your lower, fearful-self trying to sabotage your efforts, gently send it love as you would to a small child. Thank that worried or angry voice for sharing with you, then send healing light to it. In time, these darker parts of you will heal and you'll find yourself manifesting the life you desire rather than the one you fear.

# ~ Part Two ~

*Relationship Energy*

# Love Yourself

One of the problems clients come to me about most is relationship issues. They're stuck in a negative marriage, keep attracting the wrong type of partner, or have been alone for a long time. You want love and certainly deserve it, but before you focus on attracting a soulmate, be sure your self-esteem is solid. So often we're empty, bruised, battered, or broken in one or more areas and feel that if we find true love we'll heal. We believe this person will make us happy and life will be wonderful.

As we've talked about, like attracts like. If you aren't at your best you won't attract the best, no matter how badly you want it. The energy your aura puts out is a magnet attracting a person who will complement that energy.

If you were abused as a child or abused in a past relationship and haven't done inner work on this issue, you'll inevitably attract someone who will feed into your past. Almost always, you'll end up with someone who abuses you in some way.

Another odd thing happens; if you don't heal from your past and Mr. or Ms. Right came into your life, your spiritual energy will be so different from there's you wouldn't stay with the person because healthy love doesn't resonate with you. You will keep attracting what you know and what you're used to.

We all want to be happily in love, but loving yourself is a must if you want to find a person who is caring, passionate, and good for you. Every relationship you bring into your life is equal to the relationship you have with yourself.

Everything I talk about in my books comes from personal experience and having been a psychic life counselor for decades. As a child, I was raised by drug-addicted, neglectful, abusive parents. At fifteen I met my first husband and was pregnant by sixteen. Since I was used to living in an abusive household, his abuse didn't seem all that bad. How sad is that? After 17 years though the abuse got worse and I finally gathered the strength to take our five children and leave.

I thought that since I left the abusive relationship I'd now attract a wonderful man. Boy, was I wrong! Now I had a history of abusive parents, nearly two decades of an abusive marriage, and had done absolutely no internal work on myself. Soon I met another man who seemed wonderful, only to discover after we were married that he was abusive too. Big surprise, right? This time I only stuck around for seven years before getting a divorce.

Finally, I realized that to attract a man who was stable, good, caring, and loving, I needed to work on myself. And so, I did. I jumped right into healing my mind, spirit, and emotions while treating my body much healthier. Along the way, I dated but I could recognize potentially toxic relationships within a date or two and dropped those men quickly.

Ultimately, I found my Mr. Right, but something weird happened; in the beginning, I was overly cautious because he was so good and so nice! My negative love-programming ran so deep that even though I finally attracted a great guy, it went against what I was used to and comfortable with. However, because I had been working on self-love I recognized that my fear came from those old programs my mind was running. It's crazy to realize you have to teach yourself to enjoy happiness. We're all pursuing happiness, but until we love ourselves we'll avoid it at all costs or eventually ruin it.

What is self-love? It's self-esteem, self-acceptance, compassion, and love. Let's look at these.

*Self-Esteem*

Too often we base our self-esteem on what others think about us. We seek approval and validation from those around us because our opinion of ourselves is low or uncertain. When you live from a place of high self-esteem you won't care what others think of you. What you think of yourself is how high or low your self-esteem is.

For just a moment, think about yourself and allow your self-talk to run with this. You may start hearing all sorts of messages in your mind and a lot of feelings could come up. In some ways, you probably feel pretty good about yourself, but in others, you feel lacking. Also, your opinion of yourself may fluctuate with life's ups and downs.

Nobody has high self-esteem every moment of every day, but if you feel good about yourself you bounce back faster. You'll no longer blame yourself for the problems in your life, you won't take things so personally, and will take others' opinions of you with a grain of salt. With solid self-esteem, you still think highly of yourself regardless of any losses, illnesses, mistakes, or rejections.

Then some people have huge egos and always brag about themselves. This doesn't mean they have high self-esteem. On the contrary, they feel lacking in some way and cover this up by forcing how great they supposedly are onto everyone around them.

These narcissistic individuals often base their self-worth on how they look, how much money they make, their material possessions, and/or how many people they've slept with. This isn't true self-esteem because if they experience a major loss they fall apart.

Most people tend to look at their flaws and have trouble recognizing their assets. They focus on self-criticism rather than self-esteem.

*Self-Acceptance*

Although self-esteem varies daily, self-acceptance is unconditional and steady. This means you accept yourself regardless of your flaws and failures. You forgive yourself more easily and don't judge yourself harshly. Rather than comparing yourself to friends, neighbors, co-workers, or people in the media, you can appreciate your individuality. There's nobody else exactly like you in the world and you feel good about it.

You're good enough just as you are, and getting better every day.

Something interesting happens when you accept yourself: you stop worrying about what everyone thinks about you and life flows more naturally. Nothing is forced or stagnant. You feel relaxed and allow the real you to come out and be seen. No longer do you live in a state of denial, fear, or shame.

*Self-Love*

Self-love is a healthy state to live in. If this is true, why is it easy for us to love other people though so difficult to love ourselves? We believe that loving ourselves means we're selfish or arrogant, but in fact the opposite is true. The more you love yourself, the more you can love others and attract a wonderful soulmate.

When you love another person, you accept their personality and views, even if it's different from your own. You give this person your complete respect, support, acceptance, and compassion. These feelings flow easily, yet why can't we offer the same to ourselves?

It's difficult to be gentle with yourself and take care of your needs when you're under stress, feeling exhausted, or overwhelmed. We push ourselves aside as we attempt to do even more for others or tackle the situation at hand.

So how do you develop self-love? Some choose to go to therapy, while others heal through meditation and self-help books. Others find comfort in joining online forums and groups.

Learning to love yourself takes time and isn't always easy, but each day you're presented with countless opportunities to work on yourself. When negative thoughts, self-talk, or situations arise, tune into your feelings without judging them then act according to your true feelings, values, and needs.

Every time you compromise yourself, dismiss your feelings, exhaust yourself, doubt yourself, go against your values or needs, or put yourself down, you destroy self-love. Instead, commit to making healthier choices and all areas of your life will benefit.

# How We Ruin Relationships

You have the power to live the life you truly desire. We all do. Too often though we give up our inner power and focus on the demands of relationships in our lives. Relationships affect you on every level and if it's unhealthy it soon seeps inward affecting your mind, body, and spirit.

Andrea, a client of mine, had been in an abusive relationship for seven years. Although her boyfriend didn't beat her physically, he pummeled her daily with verbal abuse. Year after year she put up with this, and all the while her self-esteem got lower and lower. Not until she caught him in bed with another woman did she leave the relationship.

During her time with this man, she put on fifty pounds, became depressed, and abandoned her previous spiritual pursuits. She had even turned her back on all her friends. It's awful how so many people get steeped in a bad relationship and completely lose themselves.

This woman is intelligent and, before the abusive relationship, had high self-esteem. So where did she go wrong? Where do so many of us go wrong when it comes to love? Below I've listed ten of the most common mistakes people make when it comes to relationships, this way you can be more vigilant. If you notice one or more of these red flags pop up in your relationship or soon-to-be relationship, stand back and ask yourself if being with this person is for your highest good.

1. *Moving too fast*. Take your time to get to know a person before trusting too quickly and revealing intimate details about yourself and your life. When you first meet someone, regardless of how kind or trustworthy they seem, you really don't know them. True love takes time and shouldn't be rushed.

2. *Easy manipulation*. When your self-esteem is fragile and you aren't sure what your own wants and needs are, you become vulnerable to manipulation. Since something is lacking inside of you that you haven't made peace with, it's easy to fall for someone who may promise to fulfill those needs. In the end, it's a relationship based on false promises.

3. *Settling*. For those who are desperate to be in a relationship, it's all too easy to settle for less than you desire. Years ago, I did this very thing. I didn't like being alone, hadn't done any spiritual work, never attempted to heal my past, and so I settled on the first guy who came along. It's not something you think about though.

Since you're viewing the world through a fragile spirit you completely believe this person is the one for you and find "proof" that he/she is your soulmate. If you were honest with yourself though you'd quickly find you were simply settling.

4. *Making excuses*. Abuse in any form is never acceptable, yet so many of us make excuses and accept being treated poorly. We allow the person who supposedly loves us to put us down or put their hands on us. People treat you the way you allow them to. Once you accept disrespect it breaks down your entire spirit.

5. *Losing yourself.* It's easy to push aside your sense of self when you're a sensitive person. Whatever your partner—or even children—want of you, that's what you give. You become a chameleon, changing according to each partner's wants and needs. Soon you have no idea who you are.

Even if you're in a loving relationship, one day you wake up and no longer recognize the person staring back at you from the mirror. In a mutually respectful and loving relationship you won't be expected to give up who you are, nor should you abandon your true essence.

6. *Becoming stagnant.* Once you're in a relationship this doesn't mean you should stop growing as an individual or a couple. When people are single they typically spend time on themselves and with friends and family, only to give it all up once they're in a relationship.

It can get to the point where they become isolated and turn away from those who care about them and have their best interest at heart. This is especially true when in a relationship with an abusive or controlling partner.

7. *Being negative.* Life is never smooth 100% of the time. No matter how much money you have or how healthy you are, you'll face situations that worry you. Being consumed with negativity won't solve anything though. Rather than thinking about it and talking about it and worrying about it 24/7, take action and do something. If there's no way to fix the problem, either let it run its course or seek out a different path.

8. *Denying dissatisfaction*. If you aren't happy in a relationship you need to face it and find out what's truly wrong and if anything can be done about it. Many times, open communication, compromise, and working toward a mutual goal can fix what's broken. If your partner refuses to work on the relationship, ask yourself if this is what you really want for your life. If you're dissatisfied with yourself in some way—you'd like to eat healthier, go back to school, budget money better, etc.—rather than dwelling on it, do something about it. Act now rather than hiding problems in the closet.

9. *Thinking "if only"*. This is a negative mindset with no possible positive outcome. If only he made more money or worked out more often. If only she lost some weight or enjoyed sports.

When you get together with a person you shouldn't do it randomly. It should be something you do with clear intent and open eyes since you need to be compatible with him/her. Going into a relationship thinking this person would be great "if only" will end in failure and is a waste of time for you both.

10. *Rebound relationships*. Dating after you recently got out of a long-term relationship isn't a bad thing. Sometimes you need to get back out into the dating world and feel passionate and happy again. However, rushing into another relationship right away is a disaster waiting to happen. You need to give yourself time to clear your mind and soul of the person you were previously with.

When you've been with a person for any length of time their energy greatly affects you. This energy needs to be cleared out or you'll attract someone just like your ex—even if the person seems nothing like her/him.

By keeping your eyes open for these red flags you'll be much more able to attract a relationship that's fulfilling on all levels. Remember though that self-love and acceptance are key to living a happy life and being in a healthy relationship with someone else.

# Soulmate Relationships

There are many conflicting theories about soulmates, but what it all comes down to is what you believe in. Throughout my studies, career, and experience, I've uncovered some facts and myths about the mate of our soul.

A soulmate relationship doesn't mean there will be no problems, that it's love at first sight, the sex is mind-blowing, and you'll never have another care in the world. Another myth about soul mates is that you have only one. Imagine, out of billions of people on this planet, only having one soulmate? That would be sad, scary, and downright unfair!

When soulmates meet there's an instant familiarity. Even if on a physical level you don't notice this, your souls will. It's like your soul and theirs hug one another, remembering the bond you shared in past lives. When these feelings come to the surface you may feel you've known one another forever or you instantly click. Things happen easily and quickly between the two of you because your souls are picking up where they left off.

Soon you experience feelings of being complete, as if you've found the other part of yourself. You're riding high on a cloud of bliss—and this is where the ego kicks in. Since you experience these powerfully wonderful feelings on a soul level, the mind eventually gets involved and starts creating a whole list of expectations. Resistance sets in, feelings of doubt plague you, and disappointment runs rampant. Even so, the love is still very strong.

The reason we meet up with soulmates is to heal old karmic patterns at a soul level. Once you're healed you may move on to someone else as the relationship runs its course, or you may stay together for the rest of this life.

Since you're brought together with a soulmate to heal spiritually, it stands to reason that the person will trigger all sorts of dark things inside you. These are things you haven't looked at in a long time, may live with daily, or might not even know exist. You'll recognize if something needs to be healed when your soulmate pushes those buttons. (This does not mean an abusive relationship is something you should stick around in though if you find yourself in one.)

Healing is a difficult process often filled with pain and turmoil as time goes on. You wish your partner would change, you point fingers and blame each other. This person just doesn't get you or see things your way, and little things start annoying you. It's so very different than in the beginning when you saw their potential and their best. Now they're showing weaknesses that need to be healed, and you're doing the same.

Pay close attention to your frustrations and arguments because every soul issue *will* be triggered by a soulmate. If you hate something about your partner it's because they're bringing to the surface something you don't like about yourself or from your past.

Talking about all of this makes a soulmate relationship sound awful, doesn't it? So where is the love of your life? That happiness or passion you crave? It all begins with you. We talked about self-love earlier and this is an absolute must if you want a positive soulmate experience rather than going from one soulmate to another working through all those tough problems.

Once you acknowledge, heal, and release those areas where you lack self-worth, you can and will attract a wildly happy and passionate relationship.

The law of Spirit won't allow you to remain with a soulmate if one or both of you are not healing. If you're trying your hardest to heal and make the relationship better but your partner isn't, hopefully, you will have increased your sense of self-love enough to understand that you deserve a healthy, loving union and will seek it out.

That's why not all soulmates spend their entire lives together. Yes, the love is still there, you will never forget that person, but you each must take responsibility for personal growth. You need to strive to be your best and happiest self, and a soulmate will always bring the opportunity to see where you need to heal.

There are also soulmate relationships where both souls are already operating at a high level. When two people of this caliber meet it's usually so they can work together to better the world or others' lives in some way. These people have worked through their personal problems and are finally at a level where they can contribute the best they have to offer.

If you're looking for your soulmate, then this means you're looking for someone who will help to bring all your deepest issues to the surface where they can ultimately be healed. Becoming whole and complete isn't always an easy process. In fact, it seldom is. The rewards are worth it though since you'll finally be able to shed your old self and live a life more in tune with who you know you could truly be.

Perhaps you're already with your soulmate and you're going through some difficult times, whether in the areas of communication, intimacy, finances, parenting, or anything else. Rather than looking outward at your partner and everything they do that drives you insane, look inward and ask yourself what areas this person is forcing to the surface. What needs to be healed?

In my own relationship, when I first met him he was far different than any man I had been with. This was a good thing since I had healed some areas of my soul, though had no idea what other work needed to be done. Since he is a soulmate, I quickly found out what areas of my soul needed healing and he discovered his. There were plenty of "knee-jerk reactions" in the beginning!

Also, at that point on my spiritual path, I knew if he was pushing my buttons there was a reason. Over time we handled each problem together and we both became more confident, wiser, and more in love.

A soulmate is always a mirror of your own soul. This person is reflecting what needs to be healed inside of you. Rather than saying, "I wish he/she could be more of this or less of that," turn inward and ask yourself why their issues bother you so much. Your ego will deflect any internal speculation and do all it can to wrestle your attention back to your partner and the outside world rather than internally.

Refuse to let your ego do the guiding in life and learn to trust your soul more. When we put so many expectations on our partner to make us happy, to fulfill us in some way, to be perfect, it's the ego talking and this holds back soul healing. A soulmate can't *make* you happy, only you can make yourself happy. A soulmate can only add to your happiness.

Another thing to remember is that your soulmate is also in this life to learn their own lessons. Maybe they aren't doing a very good job of it, but that's their path and, unless they ask for help, they need to learn on their own. You're a mirror for what needs to be healed in their soul. I always thought that was interesting to think about.

In any relationship, whether as a parent, soulmate, or friend, by letting go of the ego and living from your higher self you allow compassion and understanding to lead you. Rather than getting offended, defensive, jealous, or competitive, realize that we're all here on Earth to learn lessons and everyone is doing the best they can with the tools they currently have. This is much better than allowing life and everyone in it to throw you into turmoil.

Another interesting thing happens when you live life from the level of your higher self rather than from the ego; life gets easier and you begin to understand more. You will know true freedom and bliss, and being loving and compassionate toward others will be effortless.

# Spiritual Sexuality

In life, we've come to expect that sex is only a physical act, yet experiencing a spiritually sexual connection with another person goes far beyond this. We've been conditioned by society and the media to believe that sex is only for creating life or feeling pleasure. While this is partially true, a spiritually sexual relationship is so much more filling.

When you connect with another person on this spiritual plane it transcends all you've known and raises you to a new level of contentment with yourself and the world around you. You'll also attract abundance in all forms while experiencing love and joy you never knew existed. Sounds incredible, doesn't it?

How do you reach this level though? All it takes is some time and looking at things from a different perspective. If you're currently with a partner you can, with their participation, lift your sexual relationship to new levels. If you're single, when you're brought together with a partner you'll be able to start right away at creating a spiritually sexual relationship.

*Energy Exchange*

To begin creating a spiritually fulfilling sexual experience your touch needs to be loving, gentle, and an exchange of energy. When touching your partner, visualize energy coming from your fingertips as you touch her/him. If your partner is open to reciprocating, have them visualize the same. Slowly touch your partner wherever your hands take you, allowing your energy to flow together.

You might feel embarrassed or silly doing this exercise, but keep with it since it's so rewarding. Also, your energy fields might be out of sync, but as you work together it will eventually flow smoothly. It's not something you only feel on your skin but in the center of your being. Like a warmth and excitement that's new, intensifying the sexual experience.

It's not all about the orgasm, but a desire to feel your partner in a way where your bodies become one. When you practice this exercise, strong emotions can rise to the surface that is hard to control. You may find yourself laughing, crying, even shaking—that's how intense a spiritually sexual relationship is.

There are no walls around your heart, no armor blocking your soul. At first, this much emotion can be overwhelming. It can be very intense but just go with these feelings, even if you feel uncomfortable or afraid.

Something wondrous happens when you begin to share in this type of sexual relationship with your partner, all those old wounds begin to heal and the positive emotions will become even stronger. I've known couples who have practiced this exercise and reach orgasm without having physical sex. Or, they feel so fulfilled at a deep level, physical sex isn't as important.

That's not to say that a physical relationship should be abandoned, we *are* physical beings as well as spiritual beings. Most people choose to perform this exercise once or twice a week either instead of intercourse or as a form of foreplay.

This is an especially beneficial exercise if you had abusive or very negative relationships in the past since it creates a strong aura of trust between you and your partner. It also allows you to heal your inner self and move past the pain and trauma.

The key to making this exercise work is having a partner you can truly connect with on a positive spiritual level. If you aren't sure what type of energy your partner truly holds in their soul, pay attention to how you feel after this exercise. Ideally, you should feel relaxed, at peace, overjoyed, or any number of other positive feelings.

However, if you feel uncomfortably drained, agitated, fearful, angry, or anxious, don't ignore these sensations. The soul often knows someone isn't right for us long before our mind gets the message.

# Strengthen Your Relationship

---

Being with a soulmate doesn't mean things will run smoothly all the time. Like anything in life, it takes time and effort. Think of it as a labor of love, one you must tend to daily. By following these five steps you can be sure you're doing all you can to enhance and strengthen the spiritual relationship with your partner.

1. *Time Apart.* Everyone needs personal space since it gives us time to reflect on ourselves and our lives. This doesn't mean your partner isn't enough for you, it simply means you're taking time for yourself. When you do this regularly your mind and soul expand and you experience more tranquility within yourself and your relationship.

During your alone time, you may want to pursue activities such as taking a class, going for a walk, reading a book, painting, going out with friends, or just being alone with your thoughts and meditating or exercising.

A friend of mine had been in a relationship with the same woman off and on for four years. It was clear that they were soulmates but they definitely had their karmic issues to work through. He needed just one evening a week to go out with the guys but she didn't understand this.

Her ego got in the way and fear, jealousy, and insecurity set in. They got into an argument once and she asked why he needed time alone and why she wasn't enough for him. I felt bad that she allowed her wounded ego to stand in the way of his happiness.

Soon he felt smothered and, you guessed it, they broke up once again. I'm sure they'll be back together at some point, though I hope they work on their inner issues first. The fact is, she simply couldn't understand why he needed his space. She took it to mean he didn't want to be with her, was out looking for other women, and it soon created such a rift they needed to walk away from each other.

Time apart is healthy for a relationship, just as together time is. If your relationship is strong you're never really apart since your souls are always united.

2. *Keep Romance Alive*. When a relationship is new romance and passion are at the front and center of it. We love spending every moment with this person, and everything is new and exciting. Over time though routine sets in and the spark fades. Soon, you see the relationship and your partner as boring and you both stop trying. It doesn't have to be this way though. Relationships are jobs and it takes time and effort to keep them running smoothly.

Of course, this should be done out of love rather than drudgery. No matter how little time you feel you have, or how little money, you can and should plan regular romantic evenings. Once a week is ideal. This can be dinner and a movie, a cozy dinner at home, or whatever else you can do to create more romance and passion.

3. *Mutual Activities*. Though it's healthy to spend some time apart, it's also important to find an activity you both enjoy doing and do it together. This could be gardening, hiking, volunteering, or anything else the two of you can participate in as a couple. By doing something you enjoy and sharing it with your partner it will strengthen the bond between you.

4. *Be Affectionate*. Humans thrive on loving touches. In fact, studies have shown that newborns that are often held and loved become more confident and loving adults. It should go without saying then that enjoying a deeply spiritual relationship also includes physical affection. Touch your partner often in non-sexual ways such as holding hands, a gentle shoulder massage, and many hugs and kisses.

This sharing of touch and energy can really make your day. These displays of affection keep the relationship flames alive and show your partner how much you care. Be sure to touch your spiritual partner every day, several times a day.

5. *Fix What's Broken*. Unfortunately, far too many couples run away from their relationship problems rather than trying to fix what's broken. They take the easy way out and start looking for another partner right away. The Universe brought the two of you together for a reason. You have something to learn from each other.

Remember how we talked about your partner being a mirror into your soul? What irritates you about your partner? Now, look inside yourself to see what needs healing or growing. This can also help to heal the relationship. Of course, if your partner isn't working on the relationship with you, you can only do so much. Just be sure you've done all you can before walking away.

No relationship is easy all the time, not even a spiritual relationship, but it can be a beautiful and fulfilling journey if you both try.

# Money Energy

---

This section of the book is about relationship energy and most often we tend to think of this in terms of love and finding that elusive soulmate. But we also have a relationship with money. Becoming your higher self doesn't mean you should give up enjoying the things money can buy, but it does mean you probably need a healthier relationship *with* money.

If you're struggling with finances, are in debt, and find it difficult to make your paycheck stretch, you aren't alone. In fact, relationship troubles and money troubles run neck-and-neck as the top stress factors in life. There never seems to be enough money and with no relief in sight.

But, did you know you already have everything within you to attract great wealth? If you truly desire more money this means the spiritual energy already exists within you. You can't yearn for something without the knowledge of how to attract it living inside you. If this is so, then why does it seem you're always struggling with finances?

Because, from a young age we're conditioned to believe that money is somehow evil, that it makes us greedy, materialistic, bad, or there simply isn't enough to go around. It's something to be spent as quickly as it appears. In reality, a lack of money often causes people to feel or do desperate things. It's like a constant tug of war where money is concerned!

Instead, by creating a spiritual shift within you and being in alignment with your higher self, you can embrace wealth, attract money, and do wonderful things with it. There's no reason why a person can't be both rich and spiritual. After all, spirituality is an inner path that helps you to discover your true essence, deepest values, and your personal source of inspiration.

How many of us have and still do struggle with a 40 hour per week job? You dream of a new career or even your own business, but something holds you back. Fear is what does it. Fear limits you in all areas of life, making you feel stuck and with a dreary outlook of your financial future.

Changing your current financial status starts simply. All you need to do is open your mind and heart to wealth. Refuse to dwell on it or block it. Instead, know that you deserve to be financially stable and that the only thing preventing you from achieving this success is a stubborn blockage in your energy field.

You have unlimited potential that can bring you unlimited wealth. I've proved that in my own life. Even though the economy is down, I'm making more money now doing something I love than I ever did in the past working 60 hours a week at a regular job. This isn't my ego talking, I mention this so I can inspire you and assure you that if I can do it anyone can. I wasn't born wealthy or a super genius or lucky.

For many decades, I struggled with poverty and never believed I would one day be living the life I am today. Sure, I wished for it, hoped for it, and even prayed, but deep inside I felt it was out of reach. And that's what keeps us so separated from wealth. No matter how much you want it, if you don't believe you can be financially self-sufficient it won't happen. Our desperation creates a block that refuses to allow money to flow freely to us.

You have unlimited creativity within that will guarantee a positive change in income. What does creativity have to do with money? Being creative is closely related to spiritual energy since it comes from that place deep inside, beyond the conscious and all logical thinking. Many people feel they aren't creative, though this is a false belief. We are all naturally creative.

So now you know that creativity and spirituality are closely linked and that the fastest way to increase your finances is to discover new ways to make money. How do you do this though?

*Personal Time*

No matter how hectic and packed your days are, you can surely set aside just 10 minutes, even if it's only once a week in the beginning. Think about how much time you spend online, watching TV, or on other unproductive things. Of course, you need some downtime to unwind, but just once a week—or more if you choose—take a few minutes and spend personal time on yourself. That's all it will take to begin changing your financial life.

Find a quiet place and create a space just for you. This could be a part of your bedroom, your desk, or a shelf in a corner. Place some crystals, polished stones, or other items that represent peace to you.

I have a nightstand in my room that I've set up as my "altar." Depending on how I feel and what energies I'm trying to bring into my life will dictate what I put on this table. When I want to attract more money I typically put green stones, gold-colored objects, and an affirmation that might say, "Money flows freely to me. I'm financially self-sufficient."

Whatever you decide to put in your special area, try to go here at least once a week—though doing this daily will create results faster—and enjoy quiet time. No television, radio, computer, or phones. Just sit with your eyes closed and listen to the voice within. Allow your higher self to come through and offer guidance.

You'll know when you've found this wise part of yourself because your ego won't be involved. Instead, you'll feel a sense of calm, a sense of knowing, perhaps excitement, and new ideas come to you as well. The ego is much different because it will tell you to be afraid or angry or to give up altogether.

This time away from the everyday stress and busyness of life will offer you a chance to relax, to recoup your energy and enthusiasm, and can show you new ways of doing things for your highest financial good. Soon, you'll find that inspiration and ideas will come easily. It's like your special place instantly connects you with your higher self.

*Journaling*

Whenever I tell people how powerful journaling is they tend to laugh it off and never give it a try. What a mistake! I urge you to buy a notebook—as plain or fancy as you like—and write in it every day, even for a minute or two. Open your journal and ask your higher self a question and just start writing. Yes, it's that easy! Don't think too much about what you're getting down on paper, just let it flow out of you. When you're done, you might be surprised at what you come up with.

Years ago, I wrote in my journal every day. When we're going through trying times it's comforting to have someplace to write all your thoughts down. Now I journal whenever I feel the need, which is typically when I'm at a crossroads in life.

When I was finally serious about changing my financial situation, I sat down with my journal and asked my higher self to guide me along the most lucrative yet enjoyable path. I had been doing psychic counseling and had honestly thought this path would lead to public speaking and teaching classes.

Instead, my higher-self recommended I start writing books—lots of them. At first, I didn't take this too seriously and kept going along my familiar path, but eventually, I decided to give writing a chance and it took off like wildfire. You see, your higher self will always know the best way to bring you financial abundance!

*Ideas And Action*

When people tell me they never get any ideas while meditating or going to their quiet place I tell them it's because they're trying too hard. Your life has probably been stagnant or chaotic for a long time and thinking that a brilliant idea will rise up at a moment's notice and rescue you isn't going to happen.

Instead, each time you meditate, imagine your life as a blank sheet of paper or blank canvas. Ask your higher self, guides, angels, or God to send you an idea that will help you then let the thought go. Keep your inner mind focused on the paper or canvas and see what appears. You could get a picture of an item or you may see words. Perhaps you'll get neither of those, though you'll get a strong feeling as to what you should do.

Don't worry if the item you see or words you get don't make sense at first. Trust that in time it will all come together. Once you put forth the intention to receive ideas they *will* come to you and ideas will turn into money once you act on them.

Simply put, your higher self receives ideas then your logical self takes these ideas and pursues them. This is how you get a balanced flow of energy and where the real magic happens. It really is that easy. Not everything will work out, but the more you act the more you'll find that things do pay off and you'll eventually find the pot of gold you've been searching for.

# Physical Energy

---

Spirituality and your relationship with your physical-self go hand-in-hand. Just because the body is associated with your lower Earth self doesn't mean it's any less important than your spiritual-self. Nothing is separate. If you ignore one thing it affects all others. When was the last time you felt truly healthy, vibrant, full of energy?

When people first start their spiritual journey, they get excited and steeped in all the new things they're experiencing on the mental, emotional, and spiritual levels. It often feels as if you've been on a lifelong fast and suddenly find yourself standing in front of a mouth-watering buffet! You want to dive into these new feelings and thoughts and explore them to their fullest to see where they take you. This is wonderful, though you need to pay attention to your physical body too.

Many of my clients have told me that once they started focusing on their spirituality their bodies started becoming weaker or new health problems popped up. That's because it's so easy to get distracted by the spiritual journey. When your body is strong and healthy you're more able to experience and understand your spiritual pursuits. Your body will vibrate at a higher frequency and be more in alignment with your higher-self.

*These are some tried-and-true steps to regaining physical energy:*

1. The first step is following a healthy diet. Each body is different and you need to pay close attention to what's right for you. We always know what's best for our own highest good! Just because your friend is energetic and lost weight on a raw food diet, you may need a low-carb diet containing healthy portions of meat. It's always a wise decision, regardless of which health plan you're following, to cut out sugar, caffeine, alcohol, and processed foods. Just doing that alone can make you feel so much better.

I'll go a step further and say to cut out artificial sweeteners as well. About a decade ago I was having panic attacks, migraines, constant anxiety, sleep problems, and more. Although I ate pretty healthy, I didn't realize that artificial sweeteners were the culprit! Once I cut those out all my physical symptoms disappeared.

Just cutting out what you know isn't good for you, you can gain more energy, think more clearly, even your mood can improve. I've been on too many diets to count and have found that eating as simply and as close to nature as possible works best for me: Lean meats, eggs, fresh fruits and vegetables, berries, nuts, and so forth.

Eat only when you're hungry and stop eating when you feel satisfied. Far too many of us overeat without realizing it or overeat because we're filling an emotional void. I'm even worse because I tend to overeat when I'm happy, and I'm happy quite often! If I'm sad or depressed I totally lose my appetite.

The easiest way I found to stop eating too much was to serve my meals on salad plates rather than the typical big dinner plates. My eyes see the plate as very full, though in reality, it's about half of what I used to eat. It's a simple trick that works well.

2. Get some exercise every day. Even if all you can fit in is a ten-minute walk around the block, do it! There are days when all I can fit in (or muster up) is a five-minute stretching session. *Some exercise is better than none*. Exercising brings oxygen into your bloodstream, your lungs, your cells. It helps to release blocked energy in your aura and improves your thinking, your mood, even your libido! Best of all, it's free.

3. Drink enough water. There are conflicting theories about how much water you should drink. Some experts say you should have at least half a gallon of water a day while other experts say to drink water when you're thirsty. I follow the rule of thumb that my body knows what it wants. Some days I'm thirstier than others, but I always, always have a bottle of water nearby and avoid sodas, juices, and so forth.

4. Get enough sleep. Some people need only six hours while others need nine. Most people need about eight. The truth is though, most of us don't get enough sleep or go, go, go until we're exhausted. It's that, "I'll sleep when I'm dead" way of thinking.

Your body repairs itself while you sleep so it stands to reason that without enough rest you're not operating at full capacity. Make sleep a top priority in your life and you'll find that you're more able to eat healthier, make better choices, exercise more, and continue on your chosen path.

5. Write down your goals. Whether you want to lose a respectable one pound per week, add more veggies to your diet, get in some exercise each morning before heading to work, or increase the size of your biceps, write it down. Doing so makes your goals more manageable and by seeing them in your own writing (or typing) you feel more in control, more confident, and assured of where you're going. Be sure to break your goals down into small steps and a date when you want to accomplish each step. As time goes on, revise your plan and adjust as necessary.

6. Love and accept your body. No matter where you're starting on your journey, love the body you have. It's gotten you this far and will take you even farther, especially if you start taking better care of it.

Don't feel depressed if you aren't built like an athlete or supermodel and don't hate yourself because you've neglected your physical health for so long, today is a new day! Strive to be the best you can be rather than living up to what the media says is the ideal male or female. If you feel healthy, happy, and energetic, that's what truly counts!

I haven't said anything new here, but that only goes to show that the simplest things work. The reason we're so unhealthy is because we're seeking out the magic pill, the miracle workout, or waiting for energy and inspiration to get us going. It's not going to happen so just start doing it! After a few weeks, your new routine will be a habit and nothing you have to think about since it will be natural for you to follow this healthy lifestyle.

# ~ Part Three ~

*The Big Stuff*

# Letting Go Of Fear

When you have good things in your life it's natural to fear losing them. Some fear is healthy since it can help you take steps to protect what you've worked hard to achieve—whether it's your bank account, career, health, or relationship. It only becomes unhealthy when you constantly fear losing something when you can't do anything about it. When you focus your energy on fear of loss you create what scares you most.

You can't control other people and you can't control what happens to you, but you *can* control how you react. You and you alone control your thoughts and actions. The best way to let go of fear is to change your outlook.

Everything in life is energy and this energy often becomes physical things we cling to. By shifting your thoughts from scarcity and worry to more positive thoughts like peace, love, and action, you can release fear. Whenever I sense negative feelings creeping up on me I don't react right away. Instead, I ask what the negative feeling is trying to tell me or show me. Usually, it's some wounded part of my child-self coming to the surface, or my ego trying to take over the driver's seat.

I then take a deep breath and ask myself, "How would love handle this?" If you do anything from the point of view of love you'll feel an immediate release of fear and a calmness settle over you. You'll think more clearly and make much better decisions. In turn, this will lead to more success and security in your life. We so often act out of fear that life can be a living hell at times. No fear, know peace. Pretty simple, right?

# Enjoying Your Life

---

What you think and how you act have a huge effect on your overall happiness. You want to enjoy life from the level of your higher self, but the problem is, you've been pre-programmed! By the time you're in kindergarten, you've had 50% of your mind programmed by the adults around you, and by the time you're a teenager you've had more than 2/3 of your mental, emotional and spiritual programming done by others. No wonder we walk around feeling unfulfilled, repeating the same patterns over and over again no matter how hard we try.

The key to becoming your higher self and using your spiritual energy to transform your life means you need to change your inner programming so you can enjoy life more. Sound confusing or difficult? It really isn't. I go into detail on how to change all of your programming in my bestselling book *Reprogram Your Subconscious - Use The Power Of Your Mind To Get Everything You Want*, but right now let's cover a few simple things to get you started.

*Beliefs Become Reality*

It's good to question your beliefs from time to time. Do they still serve you, or are your beliefs holding you back? As Anais Nin said, "We don't see the world as it is, we see it as we are." The way one person sees something may be totally different than how someone else sees it. You could look at the ocean and see it as being beautiful and peaceful, while someone else sees it as a horrifying death trap. And it's all due to our internal belief system.

Next time you sense anger, fear, or worry creeping up on you, look inside yourself and see what beliefs are helping to create these feelings. Where did this programming come in at? Did your parents always fight about money so now, whenever money is tight, do you become depressed or frantic? Did your first love cheat on you and now you constantly find "proof" that your current love interest is cheating?

Ask yourself if you truly need to hold on to the belief. Is it helping you in any way or simply holding you back? How much happier and freer would you be if you let it go and adopted a more positive and constructive belief system?

*Nurture Your Inner Child*

Very few of us can say we had ideal parents, or that our childhood was wonderful in every way. Each one of us has an inner child that is wounded, angry, lonely, scared, or sad in some way. By doing this exercise you have a chance to parent yourself and ultimately heal.

Find a picture of yourself as a child when you were smiling. Frame it and set it on your nightstand or hang it on a wall you pass by often. Look into the eyes of the child you were then and offer a smile in return. Send loving, healing thoughts to your child self. Talk to him/her. This might sound like a silly thing to do, but you'll be surprised at the amount of emotion that erupts when you dare to look into your own eyes.

I did this exercise myself years ago after getting out of my second dysfunctional marriage. I knew I kept choosing negative relationships because of my upbringing. My grandparents and parents had bad marriages so that's all I knew and what I mirrored in my adult life. When I looked into the eyes of my child self it was heart-wrenching and incredibly difficult to maintain eye contact for more than a few seconds. I stuck with the exercise though and over time helped to heal the child part of me and went on to find happiness.

Look at your younger self. Do you feel bad for the child in the picture? Sad? Do you feel the child is weak and pitiful and it makes you angry and disgusted just to see that face? Any negative feelings that come up are clear indications that work needs to be done, issues need to be faced, and emotions must be healed.

*Accomplish More Goals*

How many times do you fall into bed at night feeling you got nothing accomplished? There's a long list of things you wanted to do, but somehow you forgot about them, got sidetracked, or by the time you remembered you were too exhausted to care.

Make a list of your top goals for the following day. Try to include no more than five things since you don't want to feel defeated before you start. Tackle each one in turn until you've got the list cleared out. Then when you settle down to some well-deserved relaxation time, you won't feel guilty.

Do this for large projects and long-term goals too. Whether you want to go back to school, lose weight, or clean the junk out of your home, break the task down into tiny steps that are easy to follow. Pretty soon you'll accomplish what you set out to do.

*Avoid Complaining*

I say this again and again in my books, "What we focus on expands." The more you focus on the negative in your life and complain about it, the more it's going to bother you and the more difficult it will be to get rid of the problem. How can you possibly enjoy life if all you do is concentrate on what's not working?

An easy way to see how complaining strangles any hope of achieving the goal of becoming your higher self is to think of your life as a garden. Let's say you're on your knees tending to your garden but all you see are the weeds. You can't see the young plants trying to sprout since you're too busy pulling weeds and cursing them. As you complain you forget to water those young plants and soon they die.

Rather than blaming yourself for your laser-like focus on the weeds (your problems) and lack of attention to the young plants (the good things in your life) you blame your rotten-looking garden on the weeds themselves.

Your problems can't make you miserable, only your constant focus on them and inaction can. From now on, every time you catch yourself complaining—whether out loud or inside your head—stop yourself and replace the complaint with something positive. Instead of saying something like, "I'm so fat! How could anyone find me attractive?" Replace it with a positive statement such as, "I really love my eyes (or smile, or chest, or feet, or whatever.)" In time, you'll see that you're complaining less while life becomes happier.

*Have A Positive Outlook*

Don't let a bad mood or worry color your days and nights. Feelings only control your life if you allow them to. Naturally, we'd love to have positive thoughts constantly dancing through our minds, too often though we see life through the glasses of negativity or worry. When we do this, nothing seems right or good. Our problems appear insurmountable, and people seem completely impossible to get along with.

If they had a gold medal for worrying, I'd be the Olympic champion. There are times when I'm in bed awake allowing every worry—real and imagined—to parade through my mind all night long. Lately though when I catch myself in worry mode I put on the brakes and laugh at myself. After all, what in the world can I accomplish by worrying? Worrying is passive, it gets you nowhere, and it has never solved or prevented a single thing!

Then, as we talked about before, I change my worry to wonder. I ask myself, "Hmm…I wonder how I can overcome this obstacle? Maybe I could try this. If it doesn't work, I'll try something else." The following morning, I put my plan into action. Now, I'm doing something. I'm moving forward and creating change in my life rather than remaining stagnant with worry.

The next time you find yourself worrying or in a bad mood, realize that it's simply a glitch in your thought pattern at the moment. Stop yourself and change your line of thinking to that of wonder. "I wonder why my boss is in a bad mood today? Maybe he's under a lot of stress." Or, "I wonder how I can pay my cell phone bill this month? Maybe I can take the bus to work or share a ride with someone a couple times a week and save on gas money."

By changing your line of thought to that of curiosity and wonder you allow growth to take place and you reach ever-higher, ultimately becoming your true self. Give it a try when you find your mind spinning wheels. See what you can come up with that will help create changes so you can enjoy life more rather than staying in a cycle of frustration or procrastination.

# Getting What You Want

I want to share two simple steps for getting what you want in life. Whether you're trying to increase your spiritual energy to attract love, money, a career, or anything else, by doing these two things you'll find you become more and more successful as you live from a state of your higher self.

1. Create a plan of action. There's no way to be truly successful at anything if you jump in with your eyes closed or do things only halfway. If you want to get more out of life the first step is to think about what you desire most. Let's say you want to double or even triple your income. First, ask yourself why you want to make more money and be very precise about it. I wanted to make more money so I could be at home with my kids, live in a better neighborhood, and enjoy more fun times rather than just scraping by.

Once you know why you want something, create a plan of action to achieve it. Wishing alone won't make it happen. Do you need to take better care of your health, go back to school and get a higher degree, or socialize more so you can start dating and ultimately find your soulmate?

Whatever it is, make a detailed plan and start on it today! The number one reason so many people are unsuccessful and constantly live a life controlled by their lower self is because they don't have specific plans and no agenda of how to reach their goals.

2. Take action. Opportunities are everywhere so stay open to receiving them and acting on them as often as possible. It's easy to focus on what we *think* an opportunity will look like, but it rarely happens that way. Opportunities don't usually come wrapped up in neat packages and may even surprise you, so be ready to take calculated risks if something comes your way.

There's no such thing as good luck or bad luck. Those so-called lucky people are no different than you, except for the fact that they do their best to take advantage of opportunities rather than hiding in fear or denial.

Tracy, a friend of mine, kept waiting for a promotion at her job, though she was always passed over. She'd been there five years and this was really getting to her. She liked her job but felt she'd never move up the career ladder. One day as she was getting into her car she saw that someone had put a flyer on her windshield for a class on income tax preparation.

At first, she thought about tossing the paper away but remembered the conversation I had with her a few days before on being open to opportunities in even the most random places. She ended up taking the class, enjoyed it, and was hired by a popular income tax preparation company, and moved up the ladder quickly.

Now she's making four times what she did at her old job. See, if she had been closed off she would have just wadded up the paper and put it in the garbage. Instead, she took the opportunity and it paid off in a big way.

Those two things—creating a plan of action and taking action—will help you get what you want in life. One without the other won't work.

# Living Your Dreams

---

Yes, I'm saying it again: If you truly believe something it becomes your reality—good or bad. Too many of us live in a "bad reality" state of mind. Whenever I feel down or want to throw in the towel regarding my life path and dreams, I know it's just my lower self in the driver's seat. Sometimes it seems like she's on a cross-country road trip!

But, I also know that thoughts are just thoughts and in no way reality unless I make them so. Knowing that allows my higher self to take over and begin thinking positively, which keeps me moving forward.

Nearly everyone has some dream in mind that they feel is totally out of reach, yet they can't let it go. They want to lose weight, to be in a better relationship, to have a more stable financial life, to start their own business, to play a musical instrument, to go back to school, or maybe take up rock climbing. Many of these people have carried around the dream for a very long time.

The only thing stopping them from achieving their dreams is themselves. Yes, we all have obstacles and obligations, but nobody is ever backed completely into a corner with no way to move. There's always at least a tiny bit of room for movement forward.

How do you move forward when you feel crushed under the weight of your problems? I know what it's like to be in a deep hole of debt, have health problems, and unfulfilling marriage. You get to a place where you can't possibly see the light at the end of the tunnel. Even if you did, you'd think it was a train coming to run you down!

You have two choices: Spend the rest of your life buried under your problems and dream your days away, or buckle up your courage and determination and change things around. No matter how hard it is to create a better life, I'd rather try than admit defeat, and I'm sure you would too.

What do you envision for your dream life? How can you achieve it?

1. Grab a notebook and pen, or if you prefer using your computer, open a new document.

2. Give your page an empowering title like, "My life from this moment on", or, "From dreams to reality." I titled mine, "This is who I am." Having that title helps to imprint this new life into your mind since you'll read it each day.

3. Get down to work. On the first page make a list of where your life isn't working, on the next page make a list of your dreams. Each consecutive page will hold the title of one problem and one dream. So, one page may be titled: Getting out of debt. Another could be titled: Going back to school.

4. Under each title brainstorm ways to overcome the problem or make the dream into reality.

5. Take your biggest dreams and break them down into small, manageable steps, then taking action every day toward your goals. For instance, years ago I was a single mother living on only $900 a month and had 5 kids to feed, bills to pay, etc. I titled one page: *Ways to bring in extra money*. I listed as many things I could think of to make extra money without having to go out and get a regular 9-5 job and leave my kids alone all day. (I homeschooled my kids.)

I'm an avid book collector, so I figured I could sell them on Amazon. I also went to library sales, bought books for pennies on the dollar, and sold them through Amazon as well. I also started offering psychic readings on eBay. Those two things got me out of the financial hole I was in.

Of course, each of those ideas had its own small steps such as creating ads on eBay and listing the book information on Amazon, but those two ideas were the quickest, easiest, and cheapest ways to bring in money.

What about dreams? I had always wanted to be a multi-published author and had written romances since I was in my 20's, though had never been published. Those manuscripts sat around collecting dust for 15 years until I found myself divorced for a second time.

Being on my own again had me dredging up all sorts of dreams. I made a list of ways to get published. I was far too eager—and broke—to go the traditional publishing route. Printing out manuscripts, paying for postage, and waiting eons for a reply wasn't something I wanted to do.

Instead, I did extensive research into eBook publishers and sent some query letters to the top ones on my list. Since December 2007 I've signed nearly a dozen book contracts and many of my books have become best sellers. Now I self-publish all my books since I enjoy the control and the entire publishing process, plus I'm making an incredible living with my books.

Nobody goes from a minimum wage job to being wealthy in the blink of an eye, weight doesn't drop off within weeks, and a book can't be written and published in two days, but with your step-by-step plan of action and determination to follow through each day, you can't possibly fail.

The biggest obstacle to achieving what you set out to do is a lack of focus. By breaking big projects or problems down into small steps you can overcome just about anything, and begin living the life of your dreams.

Becoming your higher self and developing spiritual energy, then using it for your benefit will allow you to live a life of abundance. You *can* enjoy good health, true love, a big bank account, and so much more.

# Finding Your Life Purpose

---

I'm ending this book with a subject many of us are seeking answers to: What is my life purpose? Everyone has a life purpose, though not all of us are meant to be the next Gandhi or Mother Teresa, or Bill Gates or Johnny Depp or Oprah.

Your life purpose is something that must fulfill *you* on as many levels as possible. It should be rewarding mentally and/or emotionally and/or spiritually and/or physically. If it covers all these areas then so much the better! But, how do you go about finding your life purpose?

1. Don't compromise yourself. In other words, you can't spend your life doing for others, following someone else's path and dreams and goals, and bowing down to society. You need to be true to yourself, your wants, your needs, and your desires.

That's not to say that you should suddenly become rude or irresponsible, ditch your marriage, abandon your kids, and tear up your bills. What it does mean is that you might have to say "no" more often so you can pursue things that fulfill you and bring you peace. Maybe you want to volunteer, or simply read a book under the shade of a tree.

2. Live your life as if every day has a purpose. Rather than looking at the end result of your grand purpose in life, take each day and use it as mini-steps that will get you to where you need to be. Maybe you don't know where it is you want to end

up. That's okay! As long as you're doing things every day that bring you comfort and happiness you'll eventually find your purpose at some point.

3. Keep learning and take action. Read a book, watch a documentary, take a class, whatever you can do that will stretch your mind will help you discover your purpose. Your mind and soul are like a rubber band and every time it stretches it never goes back to the original shape. Keep stretching!

4. Remember it takes time. We spend decades screwing up our lives or remaining stagnant yet we want to be successful and live a life of purpose moments after reading the latest self-help or how-to book? It's not gonna happen! Life is a journey, not a destination. Sure, look upon your true purpose as someplace you'll eventually get to, but enjoy the scenery along the way.

A life of purpose is something that makes you feel good about being alive and it should benefit others as well since all life purpose paths touch others in some way, making their lives better. Finding your purpose in life is truly easy, it just takes time and a willingness to stay the course yet freedom enough to go where the wind takes you.

# Contact Me/Book A Reading

---

Whether your problems or concerns are in the areas of love, finances, family, career, health, education, or your path in life, I offer professional psychic counseling, and caring guidance, and solutions that work. I'll give you details, time frames, predictions, and real answers. I connect directly with your higher self and your spirit guides to help you through any situation and achieve the best possible results. No problem is too big or too small, and your questions will be answered in detail.

All readings are done via email. By offering my readings through email you'll be able to save your reading and go back to it again and again for guidance.

I look forward to reading for you!

Check out my readings, books, blog posts, and more on my website:

D[1]rKellyPsychic.com

Or email me directly at:

DrKellyPsychicCounselor@gmail.com

---

1. http://psychicreadingsbydrkelly.webs.com/psychic-readings

Printed in the USA
CPSIA information can be obtained
at www.ICGtesting.com
LVHW051304050923
757191LV00005B/715